D0229910

DORSET COUNTY LIBRARY
WITHDRAWN STOCK FOR SALE

DORSET COUNTY LIBRARY

600002173 J

KINGFISHER

First published 2011 by Kingfisher
an imprint of Macmillan Children's Books
a division of Macmillan Publishers Limited
20 New Wharf Road, London N1 9RR
Basingstoke and Oxford
Associated companies throughout the world
www.panmacmillan.com

Illustrations by: Peter Bull Art Studio

ISBN 978-0-7534-3039-2

Copyright © Macmillan Children's Books 2011

All rights reserved. No part of this publication may be
reproduced, stored in or introduced into a retrieval system,
or transmitted, in any form or by any means (electronic,
mechanical, photocopying, recording or otherwise), without
the prior written permission of the publisher. Any person who
does any unauthorized act in relation to this publication
may be liable to criminal prosecution and civil claims for damages.

1 3 5 7 9 8 6 4 2

1TR/0411/WKT/UNTD/140MA

A CIP catalogue record for this book is available from
the British Library.

Printed in China

This book is sold subject to the condition that it shall not,
by way of trade or otherwise, be lent, resold, hired out,
or otherwise circulated without the publisher's prior consent
in any form of binding or cover other than that in which it
is published and without a similar condition including this
condition being imposed on the subsequent purchaser.

Picture credits

**The Publisher would like to thank the following
for permission to reproduce their material.
(t = top, b = bottom, c = centre, l = left, r = right):**
Pages 4cr Shutterstock/Ilja Masik; 4bl Shutterstock/Stanimir Dimitrov
Aleksiev; 5tl Shutterstock/Petr Masek; 5tr Shutterstock/Kevin Eaves;
5bl Corbis/Edith Held; 5br Shutterstock/Johan Swanepoel;
5brr Shutterstock/Lockenes; 6tl NASA/Apollo Program; 8cr Science
Photo Library (SPL)/Planetobserver; 8bl Photolibrary/Douglas
Peebles; 9tl Shutterstock/Monkey Business Images; 9tr Shutterstock/
Netfalls; 9bl Alamy/Design Pics Inc.; 9c Shutterstock/Jim Guy;
9br Shutterstock/Petr Masek; 10tl Corbis/moodboard;
12bl Shutterstock/juliengrondin; 12bcl SPL/Anakaopress/Look
at Science; 13tc Photolibrary/ Comstock; 13cr Photolibrary/Cusp;
13l Getty/Kevin Schafer; 13br Shutterstock/maksimum; 14bl SPL/
Kenneth Libbrecht; 16bl Shutterstock/Przemyslaw Skibinski;
16br Corbis/Henry Georgi; 17tl Shutterstock/claudio zaccherini;
17tll Corbis/Zhouming Liang; 17cr Alamy/Judith Colllins;
17bl Shutterstock/kwest; 17br Frank Lane Picture Agency (FLPA)/
Norbert Wu/Minden; 18tl SPL/Susumi Nishinaga; 20cr Shutterstock/
Rostislav Glinsky; 20bl Corbis/John Warbuton-Lee/Nigel Pavitt;
21tr Shutterstock/Jason Cheever; 21bl Getty/AFP; 21tr
Alamy/Arcticphoto; 22bl Getty/Taxi; 24cl Shutterstock/Asier
Villafranca; 24cr FLPA/ Cyrill Ruoso; 24crbk Shutterstock/
David Gallaher; 24b Shutterstock/ Mark Lundborg; 24bbk
Shutterstock/Tyler Olson; 25tr FLPA/Harri Taavetti; 25cl
Photolibrary/Alaskastock; 25br Getty/Georgie Holland; 26bl
Shutterstock/Belinda Pretorius; 28tr Corbis/Amana; 28cr
Shutterstock/Faraways; 28bl Shutterstock/ollirg; 29tr
Shutterstock/Ian Bracegirdle; 29c Corbis/Frans Lanting; 29bl
Shutterstock; 29br SPL/Martin Bond; 30tl Shutterstock/palko72;
30cbl Corbis/Patrick Robert; 30bl Corbis/Reuters; 30br Royal
Geographical Society; 31tl Corbis/Everett Kennedy Brown; 31ctr
Photolibrary/Peter Arnold Images;

Contents

More to explore

On some of the pages in this book, you will find coloured buttons with symbols on them. There are four different colours, and each belongs to a different topic. Choose a topic, follow its coloured buttons through the book, and you'll make some interesting discoveries of your own.

For example, on page 6 you'll find an orange button, like this, next to the picture of Earth. The orange buttons are about forms of life.

Page 22

Life

There is a page number in the button. Turn to that page (page 22) to find an orange button next to another example of life on Earth. Follow all the steps through the book, and at the end of your journey you'll find out how the steps are linked and discover even more information about this topic.

Science

Environment

People

The other topics in this book are science, environment and people. Follow the steps and see what you can discover!

Our planet, our home

What do people mean when they talk about our planet? Well, they mean the huge ball of rock and other material that we all live on. Our planet – Earth – is the only one we know of that is home to living things.

Water covers two-thirds of Earth's surface. Most of this water is salty water, held in the oceans.

Boats allow people to cross the oceans.

Earth, like all planets, is shaped like a ball.

This is the Atlantic Ocean, close to Central and South America.

Earth, seen from space

Earth has been photographed by satellites in space. This photo shows blue oceans, green land and yellow-brown mountains. From space, all clouds look white.

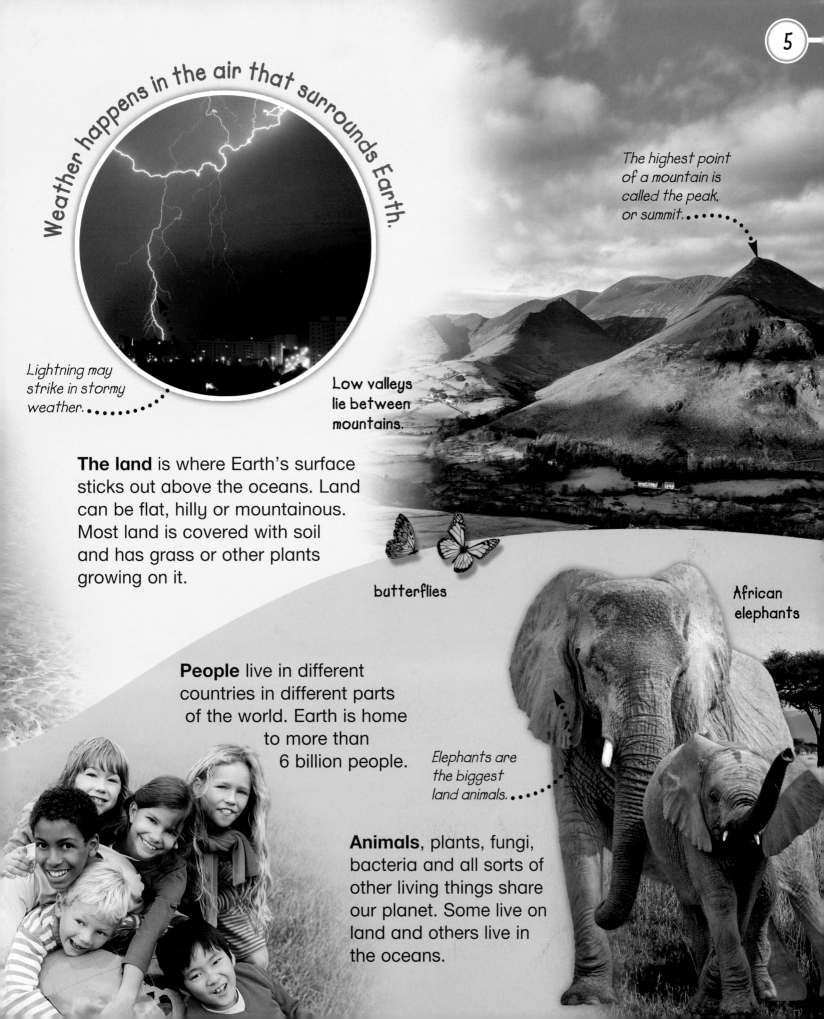

Weather happens in the air that surrounds Earth.

Lightning may strike in stormy weather.

The highest point of a mountain is called the peak, or summit.

Low valleys lie between mountains.

The land is where Earth's surface sticks out above the oceans. Land can be flat, hilly or mountainous. Most land is covered with soil and has grass or other plants growing on it.

butterflies

African elephants

People live in different countries in different parts of the world. Earth is home to more than 6 billion people.

Elephants are the biggest land animals.

Animals, plants, fungi, bacteria and all sorts of other living things share our planet. Some live on land and others live in the oceans.

1

2

Page 22

Earth in space

Earth is one of billions of objects in space. Our planet circles around the Sun, and the Moon circles around our planet. The Sun is actually a star, one of millions in our galaxy. Our galaxy is called the Milky Way. There are many millions of galaxies in space.

3

6

Earth moves around the Sun in an oval-shaped path called an orbit. There are seven other planets orbiting our Sun too. Scientists use satellites like the one below to help them investigate the wonders of space. They take photographs and gather other information. Scientists are still looking for signs of life on other planets.

5

4

Page 27

This photograph shows pits, called craters, on the surface of the Moon.

Earth, Sun and Moon

The Sun and Moon affect many things that happen on Earth. For example, the Sun gives us light and warmth, which most living things need to survive. The Moon affects the oceans, causing tides.

Sun

Here it is night-time.

Earth spins round and round as it orbits the Sun. It takes 24 hours, or one day, to complete each turn. Parts of Earth facing the Sun receive daylight. In parts that are facing away, it is night.

Earth spins on a tilt.

Here it is daytime.

Plants have leaves to help catch sunlight.

Sunlight is very important for life on Earth. Plants need sunlight to grow, and they provide us and many animals with food. The Sun also warms our planet. It drives the winds, rain and other types of weather too.

Children pick vegetables in Hawaii, USA.

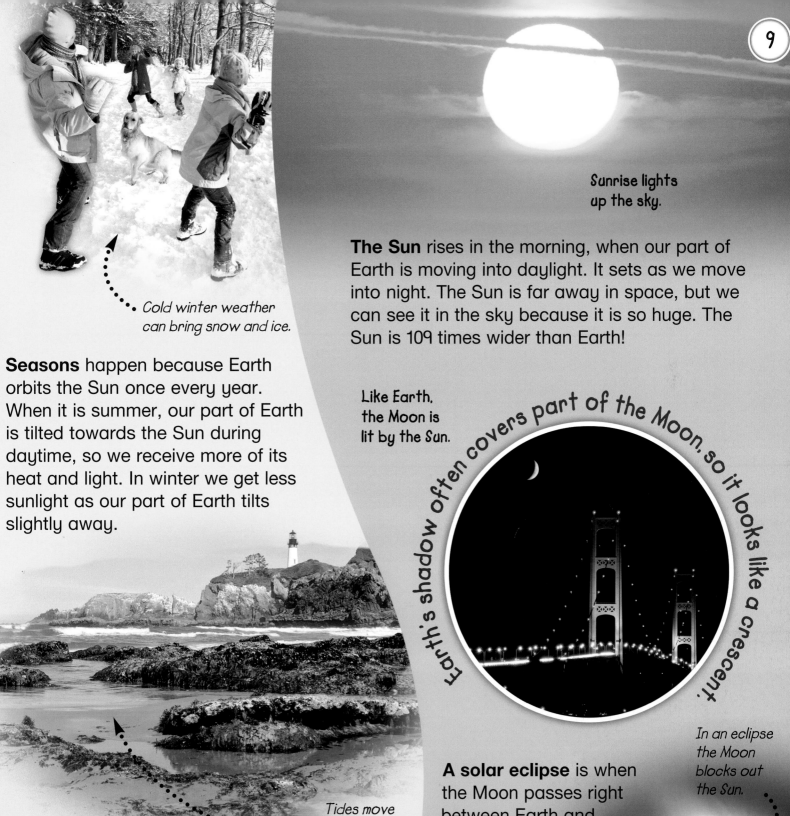

Cold winter weather can bring snow and ice.

Sunrise lights up the sky.

The Sun rises in the morning, when our part of Earth is moving into daylight. It sets as we move into night. The Sun is far away in space, but we can see it in the sky because it is so huge. The Sun is 109 times wider than Earth!

Seasons happen because Earth orbits the Sun once every year. When it is summer, our part of Earth is tilted towards the Sun during daytime, so we receive more of its heat and light. In winter we get less sunlight as our part of Earth tilts slightly away.

Like Earth, the Moon is lit by the Sun.

Earth's shadow often covers part of the Moon, so it looks like a crescent.

Tides move up and down the beach.

Tides in the ocean are caused by the Moon. As the Moon moves around Earth, it pulls the water on Earth's surface towards it. Twice every day, the sea moves away from the shore and back in again.

A solar eclipse is when the Moon passes right between Earth and the Sun. The Moon is much smaller than the Sun, but it looks the same size because it is closer to us.

In an eclipse the Moon blocks out the Sun.

Page 18

Volcanic eruption!

There are few natural sights as spectacular as a volcanic eruption. Smoke, ash and scorching lava pour out of the Earth, causing chaos and destruction. People living near active volcanoes must be ready to escape at any time.

3

Page 19

5

The people of this farming village are being evacuated to safety, as rivers of red-hot lava pour towards their homes. When a volcano erupts, lava can burn down houses. Ash fills the air and covers buildings and land. Eruptions can go on for days, weeks or even years. Their effects often spread for many kilometres around.

4

Page 15

6

This is a close-up view of lava with a cooled, hardened crust on top.

Inside Earth

Earth is made up of different layers. On the outside is the crust, where we live. Inside it is much hotter, sometimes so hot that the rocks are liquid. The sizzling centre of Earth is called the core.

Earth's crust is between 5 and 50 kilometres thick. It is made up of sections called plates, which float on the mantle beneath.

The temperature of lava ranges from 700 to 1,300°C.

Land and oceans lie on Earth's crust.

outer core

inner core

lower mantle

upper mantle

Liquid rock inside Earth is called magma.

Lava is liquid rock that has burst through Earth's crust, usually from a volcano. When lava cools, it hardens and becomes solid. The rock it forms is called igneous rock. There are two other main types of rock: sedimentary and metamorphic.

A volcanologist studies lava from a volcano.

An earthquake takes place when two plates in Earth's crust jerk suddenly against each other. This causes the ground to shake.

Valuable stones and metals are hidden in Earth's crust. In some places people dig holes, called mines, to find them.

Gold is a precious metal found in some rock.

Earthquakes happen along fault lines like this, where two plates meet.

This crown is made of gold and jewels.

This is the San Andreas fault in California, USA.

The jewels are stones dug from Earth's crust.

Fossil fuels, such as oil and coal, also come from Earth's crust. They lie in sedimentary rocks – rocks made from mud, sand or other sediments that were buried in the past.

An oil rig drills for oil in rock under the ocean.

Mountain adventure

Earth has areas of land and sea, and the land has many forms. Mountains are huge, steep-sided rock masses that rise up from Earth's crust. They are found where plates in the crust have crashed together, pushing up giant folds of rock. The tops of mountains are the highest places on our planet.

Page 30

What is this?

1. Loose snow falls in an avalanche.

2. valley made by a glacier, or river of ice

3. distant mountain peaks

This is a magnified snowflake. All snowflakes have six points and every one is slightly different.

Page 23

These climbers are on a slope in the Himalayas – the highest mountain range on Earth. Up here it is cold and windy and the air is thin, making it difficult to breathe. Mountaineers take special equipment and clothing to help them survive.

Page 19

4 Mountain peaks are often above cloud level.

5 Climbers use maps and satellite devices to find their way.

6 An oxygen tank and mask help climbers to breathe.

On the map

Maps are pictures that mark out places on Earth's surface. On world maps like this one we can see both land and sea. Maps can give us lots of information, including how high the land is and where different countries and cities are found.

Continents are the main land masses on Earth. Here the seven continents are shown in different colours.

Islands are areas of land that are surrounded by water. The photograph below shows an island in French Polynesia.

On a map, French Polynesia is here. It lies in the Pacific Ocean.

NORTH AMERICA

SOUTH AMERICA

N

W   E

S

A compass rose shows us directions: North, South, East and West.

Alps

Mountain ranges are drawn as symbols on this map. The tallest are the Himalayas in Asia. This skier is in the Alps, a mountain range in Europe.

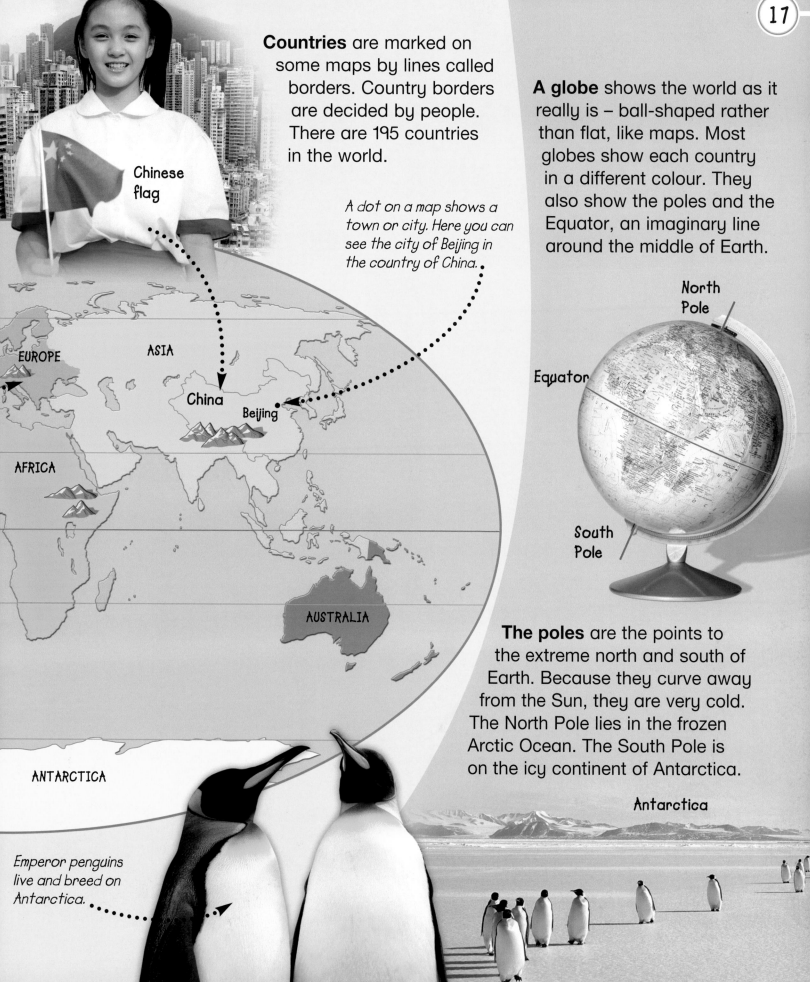

Countries are marked on some maps by lines called borders. Country borders are decided by people. There are 195 countries in the world.

Chinese flag

A dot on a map shows a town or city. Here you can see the city of Beijing in the country of China.

A globe shows the world as it really is – ball-shaped rather than flat, like maps. Most globes show each country in a different colour. They also show the poles and the Equator, an imaginary line around the middle of Earth.

EUROPE

ASIA

China

Beijing

AFRICA

AUSTRALIA

North Pole

Equator

South Pole

ANTARCTICA

The poles are the points to the extreme north and south of Earth. Because they curve away from the Sun, they are very cold. The North Pole lies in the frozen Arctic Ocean. The South Pole is on the icy continent of Antarctica.

Antarctica

Emperor penguins live and breed on Antarctica.

Page 23

1 seabirds on a cliff 2 harbour 3 cave 4 cliff

What is this?

All at sea

Most of the water on Earth is held in the oceans and seas. The area where land meets the sea is called the coast. The sea is powerful, with its moving tides and crashing waves. It slowly wears down the land, forming natural arches, cliffs and caves.

Page 30

5

6

Page 26

The coast is a lively place. Lots of animals make their homes here, and many people like to live by the sea. Some people, such as fishermen, do their jobs out on the water. In this picture a fishing boat is bringing its catch back to harbour as the Sun rises in the morning.

8

7

This is a close-up view of grains of sand. Sand is rock, broken down by waves.

Watery planet

Water can be found all over our planet. As well as in the sea there is water in lakes, rivers and ponds. Ice is frozen water and it covers large areas of land. Some water falls as rain, and some is underground.

Water vapour rises.

Water evaporates.

Rivers flow into the sea.

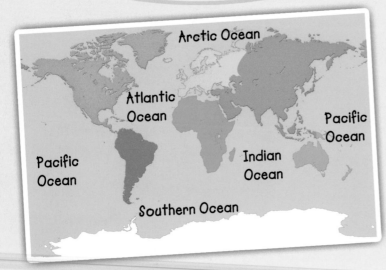

Arctic Ocean

Atlantic Ocean

Pacific Ocean

Pacific Ocean

Indian Ocean

Southern Ocean

Rivers are full of fresh water and flow across the land.

The River Seine runs through Paris, France.

Salty sea water fills the world's oceans. The three biggest oceans are the Atlantic Ocean, the Indian Ocean and the Pacific Ocean. The Pacific Ocean is the biggest of all.

People fish on Lake Victoria.

Lakes are large areas of water surrounded by land. Most lakes are full of fresh water. Lake Victoria in Africa is one of the biggest lakes in the world.

Clouds
form.

Rain
falls.

*Some water sinks into the ground
and is stored among soil and rock.*

The water cycle is the movement of
water around our planet. Heat from the
Sun evaporates water from the surface
of lakes and the sea, and it rises as water
vapour. As it is pushed over high ground it
turns into clouds and falls as rain. It then flows
back down streams and rivers to the sea.

*Rain can
fall heavily
sometimes!*

*A glacier flows
down a mountain
valley in Canada.*

*Glaciers are like rivers
of ice. They flow very
slowly downhill.*

Ice covers the land in the
world's coldest places. Many
mountain peaks have caps of
snow and ice, and ice flows
down the valleys between
them in glaciers. Ice also
covers large areas of land
near the poles.

*These dogs are pulling
a sled over ice near
the North Pole.*

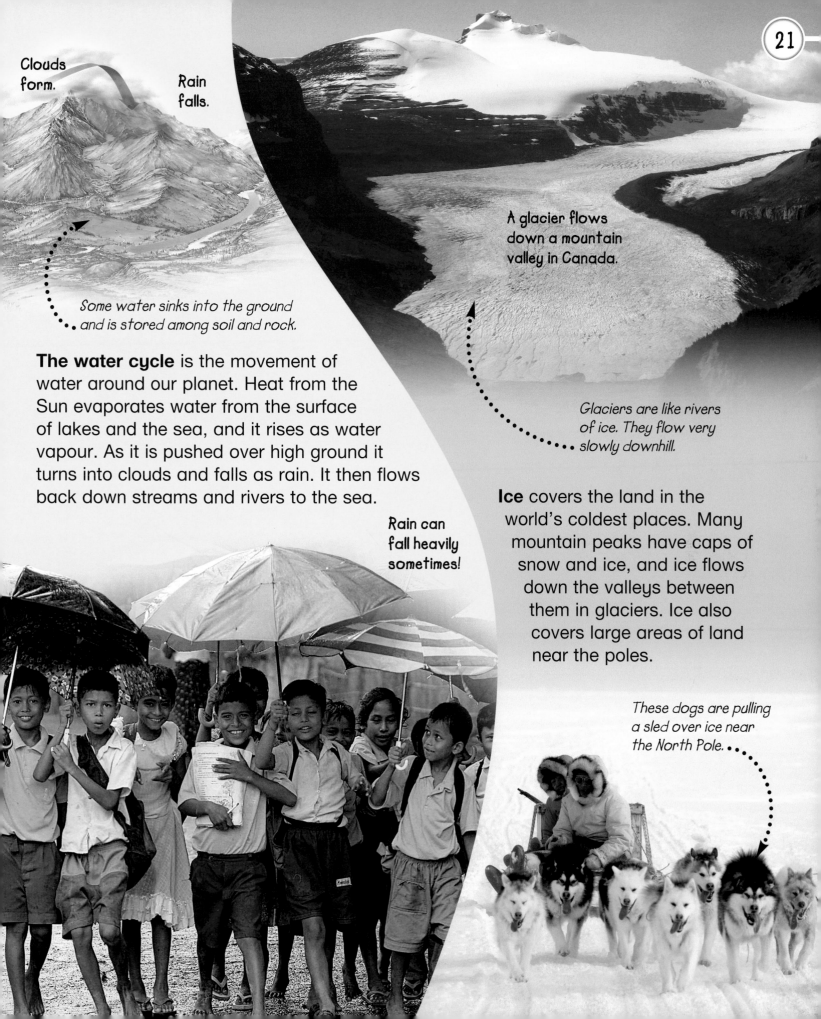

Exploring the rainforest

Tropical rainforests are full of life. They are home
to thousands of different kinds of plants and animals.
Rainforest trees are some of the tallest on Earth.
The biggest are over 60 metres high. Their
branches are thickest at the top, forming
what is known as the canopy.

What is this?

Page 11

1 boa constrictor   2 tarantula   3 scarlet macaw   4 fruit bat

? This is a tree frog's foot. Tree frogs have sticky pads on their toes to help them grip branches.

At the end of the day, a group of scarlet macaws flies in to roost in a rainforest tree. Scarlet macaws are a type of parrot and they live in South America. All around them, other animals and birds fill the treetops. Some eat leaves or fruit, but others – like the boa constrictor – are hunters that eat other animals.

Page 14

Page 30

5 three-toed sloth   6 spider monkey   7 toucan   8 tree frog

Different biomes

A biome is a type of natural habitat – a place where particular kinds of plants and animals live. Tropical rainforest is a well-known biome, but there are many others too.

Deserts are very dry places where it is tough for life to survive. Even so, they have their own plants and animals. Snakes and lizards are particularly common here.

Giraffes roam on savannah lands.

This thorny devil can go for a long time without water.

Temperate grassland is found in cooler countries, outside the tropics. In many places it has been turned into farmland and it is now one of Earth's rarest biomes.

Bushes grow among the dry grass.

Prairie dogs live on temperate grassland in the USA.

Savannah is the name given to open grassland in Africa and other hot parts of the world. It is home to herds of grazing animals and the creatures that feed on them.

A brown bear claws a forest pine tree.

Coniferous forest is made up of trees such as pine and fir, which have needles instead of large leaves. It covers large areas of Canada, Scandinavia and Russia.

Most conifers have tall, straight trunks and downward-pointing branches.

Tundra is the biome nearest the poles. This is tundra in summer.

Tundra plants are small and low-growing.

Oceans and seas are home to more living things than any of the biomes on land. They are also the least explored parts of our planet. Less than 10 per cent of the ocean floor has been properly mapped, and much of the ocean is too deep for human divers to survive.

Coral reefs like this are found in shallow, tropical waters.

Yellow angelfish

Using the land

Imagine the world without any people. It would look very different! People have changed the landscape on Earth in many different ways. We have cut down trees, dug mines in the ground, made fields for farming and built homes and roads. Every day we change our planet a bit more.

Page 30

What is this?

?

1 A plough digs up the soil.

2 logs from a planted forest

3 quarry of stone for building

This is water flowing from a hydroelectric dam. Water turns turbines in the dam to make electricity.

Page 15

This farmer is ploughing a field for crops to be planted. Crops and farm animals, like the cows in this valley, provide most of the food we eat. In the background we can see logging in a forest and diggers in a quarry. The wood and stone from these will be used for building.

4 a town in the distance

5 hydroelectric dam

6 A reservoir stores water.

7 Wind turbines make electricity.

Earth and us

Every one of us has an impact on our planet. The homes we live in and the roads and railways we travel on have changed the natural landscape. People have removed forests and other habitats to create building space as well as farmland for our food.

Villages and towns are small built-up areas of houses and other buildings. Cities are larger and cover greater areas of land. Some of the biggest cities are home to millions of people.

Ports are coastal towns built for shipping.

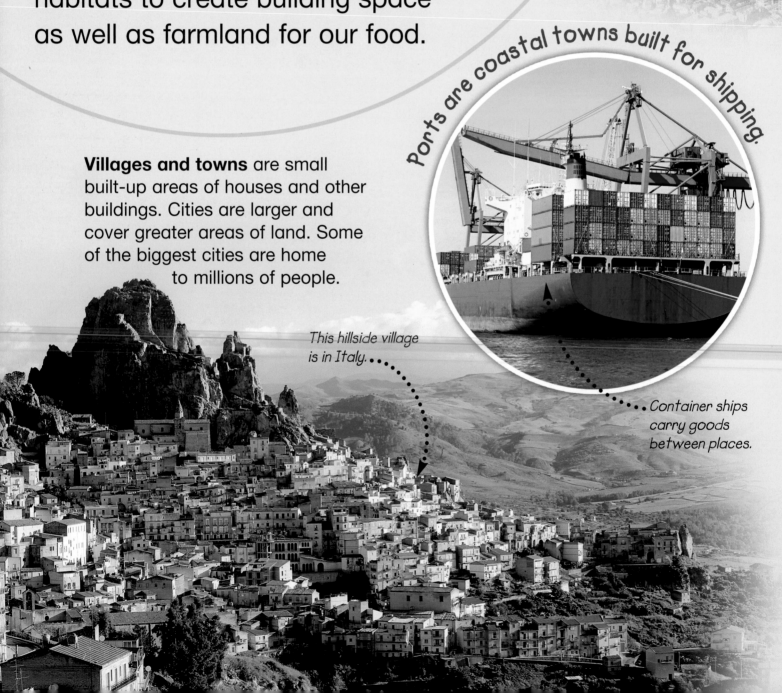

This hillside village is in Italy.

Container ships carry goods between places.

People are destroying many of Earth's **natural habitats**. As rainforests are cut down for timber and farmland, the animals that lived in them are left without a home.

Orang-utans need forests.

Tokyo is the world's largest city and the capital of Japan.

Every country in the world has a **capital city**. This is usually where the government is based.

Trains provide us with high-speed travel.

These cooling towers are part of a coal-fired power station.

Pollution happens when we burn coal and other fossil fuels. Power stations, industry and motor vehicles all create polluting greenhouse gases. These contribute to global warming, which is melting ice at the poles and causing sea levels to rise.

Transport networks run between our villages, towns and cities so that we can get from place to place. Trains cross the land on railway lines. Cars and trucks use roads, which also cut through the landscape.

Solar panels and wind turbines make electricity without pollution.

Solar panels use energy from the Sun to create power.

flamingos, zebras and a wildebeest

Rainforests are home to thousands of different living things. They all have their own place and way of life. Bats and many other creatures are **nocturnal** (active at night), and others are active in the daytime.

Life

Earth is the only place in the Universe where we know life exists. Earth is home to millions of different **species** (types of living thing). The animals above are species from East Africa.

Science

This **satellite** is helping to map the Moon's surface. Other satellites are sent into orbit around Earth. They are used for everything from sending TV signals to forecasting the weather.

Building **dams** across rivers creates artificial lakes, called reservoirs. These provide our towns and cities with water. Turbines in the dams produce electricity.

Environment

Volcanic eruptions completely change the landscape. Ash covers the ground and can crush or bury houses. Lava burns whatever it touches, then cools to form solid rock.

Cliffs look solid but bits often break away as waves pound them. This process is called **erosion** and it can change the shape of a coastline over time.

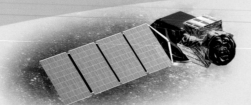

arch

People

Java (in Indonesia) is the most densely populated island in the world and it is dotted with volcanoes. Many of its 130 million people are farmers, growing rice in the rich volcanic soil.

The first people to climb the world's tallest mountain, **Everest**, were Sir Edmund Hillary and Tenzing Norgay in 1953. The youngest person to climb it was 15-year-old Ming Kipa in 2003.

Hillary and Norgay

More to explore

Volcanic ash forms rich soil that is perfect for growing crops. All plants need minerals and other natural nutrients in order to grow. Soil near volcanoes is particularly rich in these minerals.

seagulls

Coastal cliffs and islands may look bare and lifeless, but they provide nesting places for all sorts of **seabirds**. Here they are safe from ground-living hunters such as foxes, which might otherwise eat the chicks or eggs.

As altitude (height above sea level) increases, the amount of **oxygen** in the air goes down. Most climbers wear breathing equipment in high mountains to make sure they have enough oxygen.

Rainforest plants have given us many different **medicines**. One reason for protecting rainforests is to protect their plants so that scientists can continue to study them.

Rainforests are important to the **environment** because they help to balance gases in the air. Plants take in carbon dioxide, a gas that can be harmful if there is too much of it. They give off oxygen, which all animals need to breathe.

rainforest plant

In **high mountain ranges**, temperatures are very cold. The water here is frozen. Glaciers are frozen rivers that change the landscape very slowly over time. The heavy ice grinds away at the ground and forms a U-shaped valley.

Fishing is an important industry for many coastal towns and villages. The people who work on fishing boats often work through the night and they may be away for days at a time.

Most **farmers** do particular jobs at certain times of the year. Ploughing takes place in autumn or early spring, depending on the type of crop to be planted.